Doodlings & Doggerel

Doodlings & Doggerel

Sixty poems in reflective doodles

David A. Campton

New City

First published in 2022
in Great Britain by
New City

© 2022 David A. Campton

Graphic design Sandor Bartus

British Cataloguing-in-Publication Data:
A catalogue record for this book is available from the
British Library

ISBN 978-1-905039-54-8

Typeset in Great Britain by
New City, London

Printed and bound by Books Factory

Contents

Introduction 9

Before Anything Was 11
The Ballad of the Big Fish 12
The Mirror 14
Cracked Pot 15
Eternity's Mark 16
The Eighth Day 17
Listening to the Word 18
An Older Song 19
Jonah's Story, Jonah's God 23
Wakey, Wakey 25
Crying in the Wilderness 26
Isaiah's Mountain 28
Kingdom Characteristics 30
Ponder 31
Born of water and blood 32
Bethl'em Road 34
The Work of Christmas – Continued 36
Not So Good News 38
Epiphany Gifts 40
Outside is the Garden 41

Companions on a Journey	42
The Fig Tree	43
I Love You	46
Through My Eyes	48
The Theatre of God's Glory	50
Sea and Star	51
A Feather on the Breath of God	52
Frankie's Prayer	53
Beyond the Grey Sky	54
I Believe	55
The Dawning of the Day	56
A Trinitarian Creed	58
Poetry and Prayer	60
Guilt and Gratitude	61
Dust on the breeze	62
The Fixer	64
Domestic Drama	65
Aerial Battle	66
Wagtail	66
For Claudia	67
Protestare	68
That Kingdom	70
Lustily and With Good Courage	70
Joy	71
Homeless	72
Where do Poems Grow?	74
Carefully Chosen Words	76

Makers	78
Poems and Ploughshares	79
Omphalos	80
Omphalos II	81
Squaring the Circle	82
Building a City of Grace	83
Death of a Pastor	84
Reduced	89
Loss and Gain	90
Haven	92
All	94
Ride On	96

Prophet Poets

Dedicated to St Photina

With words shaped by the Living Word
Prophet poets become
Incarnate poems
Offering new possibilities,
Metaphors of the metaphysical,
Windows into the eternal,
Enabling others
To become more
Than they had ever imagined,
But everything they have always been.

Introduction

The dedication of the poem on the opposite page refers not to the first century saint, reputed to be the Samaritan woman with whom Jesus talked by a well in John 4, but my friend, a former President of the Methodist Church in Great Britain, Rev. Michaela Youngson who uses that name as her twitter handle. She is a prophet poet herself but this poem is essentially a distillation of her sermon at an Ordination Service in Cork on June 16th 2019 towards the end of her term in office.

In turn this poem prompted the creation of this anthology. I hadn't realised how many poems I had written over the years. I have posted many of them piecemeal on my blog 'Virtual Methodist' but I decided to pull 60 of them together, reworking some and discarding the most embarrassingly juvenile, which sadly weren't all written when I was juvenile. I have called it 'Doodlings and Doggerel' because I am under no allusions as to the quality of my work. Real poets would have good reason to discount much of what is here as what Stephen Fry, in his 'how to write poetry' book 'The Ode Less Taken' describes as 'the unmade bedsheets' of undisciplined art, shaped more by meaning than metre. I was never formally taught how to write poetry, beyond a rudimentary understanding of rhyme and rhythm, and the torture that was 'poetry appreciation' (indeed my O-Level English teacher Jenny Gibson, used to despair with me obsessing over the meaning of poetry whilst ignoring the building blocks of form).

However, I have always found poetry to be a helpful medium for reflection and given that I am more reactive than reflective any such discipline is useful. So many of the pieces here find their origins as reflective doodles.

Any proceeds from this are going to Copelands, an elderly/dementia care facility in Millisle, Northern Ireland. It is an initiative of Belfast Central Mission, the Methodist social care agency of which I am currently the superintendent, and which celebrated its 130th anniversary in 2019. I compiled most of this anthology during a four-month sabbatical from that post over the summer of that year, and I also completed a three-day fundraising walk from the site of a former BCM residential home, Castlerocklands in Carrickfergus, to the site of the new facility. Before the development of Copelands, this was previously a children's home run by BCM called Childhaven, and the story of this site, and my walk prompted one of the last poems in the book. Since starting this during my sabbatical a worldwide pandemic has occurred. None of these poems reflect that fact, but I hope they remain relevant, and perhaps a volume of pandemic poems may follow!

Thank you to all who have made this book possible and have encouraged (or at least not discouraged me) in my poetic endeavours over the years. Special thanks go to my ever-supportive wife Sally, and our two wonderful sons, Owain and Ciaran, who have grown into compassionate and creative young men. When did that happen?

Before Anything Was

From Genesis: A Celebration of Creativity

Before anything was I am.
Before the beginning I always had been.
I was in the beginning and the beginning was in me
As is the end.
There was never nothing,
There is always me
And always will be.
I am –
Eternally infinite,
Uncreated creator,
Unchangeable,
Yet unfathomable.
I am
But I chose to say 'Let there be...'
And there was...
There is.

A short poem written originally as the opening words of an event in the Waterfront Hall for the 10th Anniversary of New Irish Arts, based on the opening chapter of Genesis and was billed as 'A Celebration of Creation and Creativity.'

The Ballad of the Big Fish

After Amergin

I am the fish: that leaps the weir,
I am the river: from moor to mouth,
I am the cloud: that lours above,
I am the rain: the tears of the sun,
I am the gull: soaring and strutting,
I am the seedling: in crack and crevice,
I am the hillsides: embracing the city,
I am the Word: bringing all into being
In whom all things hold together.

I am the car: rushing on by,
I am the bike: crossing the bridge,
I am the lights: dictating the traffic,
I am the sun: looking down on all,
I am the boat: bound for abroad,
I am the waves: on which it sails,
I am the wind: blowing where it wills,
I am the breath: bringer of life
Hovering over the chaos.

The Ballad of the Big Fish was originally written as a performance poem for an event as part of the 2017 'Sacred in the City' Conference in Belfast that I wasn't able to deliver. It's inspired by/stolen from 'The Ballad of Amergin', reputed by different experts to be the earliest poem to have emanated from Ireland/the British Isles/Western Europe/the world – take your pick depending on the expert you prefer. It is also shaped by Colossians 1, John 1, Genesis 1, a sculpture on the banks of the Lagan in Belfast, known as the Big Fish (beside which it was ultimately delivered on the 'Wonderful Wander' as part of the 2020 4 Corners Festival) and the city in which it stands.

I am the fire: of every hearth,
I am the roof: for every head,
I am the bread: on every table,
I am the queen: of every hive,
I am the heart: of every creature,
I am the womb: of every life,
I am the tomb: of every hope.
I am the beginning and the end
And every step of the journey in between.

I am...

The Mirror

From Genesis: A Celebration of Creativity

Have you ever looked at yourself
in the mirror of a morning
And wondered 'What does anyone
see in me?'

The Creator looked at himself
in a mirror one morning,
A mirror which he had made,
A mirror fashioned out of clay
Transformed into flesh, blood and bone.
And in the mirror of man's eye
God saw himself...

But it was not good,
for He was alone
And God was never alone.
He was always 'us'.

So God made another
to make the picture complete.

And that morning he saw himself
in the mirror of humanity
Male and female,
Loved and loving,
Created to create
Together.

This was written originally as a performance piece for the 10th Anniversary of New Irish Arts and was based on Genesis 1: 26-28.

Cracked Pot

After 2 Corinthians 4: 7

Cracked, clay pot,
moss-covered,
containing
hard cold earth,
whilst beneath
the surface sits
a seed-stored life
waiting...

This short piece is one of the oldest poems here, written while working in Wicklow Methodist at the outset of my final year as a ministerial student in September 1993, based on 2 Corinthians 4: 7 where Paul writes: 'we have this treasure in jars of clay to show that this all-surpassing power is from God and not from us.'

Eternity's Mark

With thanks to Soren Kierkegaard

May I perceive in my enemy,
God's image,
in the unlovely and unlovable;
my own reflection
in the poor and the oppressed;
Christ's presence
in the powerful and oppressors;
his fingerprints;
and in everyone,
those nearby and far off,
like me, and unlike me,
those who like me
and those whom I don't like,
eternity's mark.

Prompted by Soren Kierkegaard who said '…the neighbour is eternity's mark on every human being.'

The Eighth Day

From Genesis: A Celebration of Creativity

On the eighth day the Lord arose;
and the work goes on,
with us, his apprentices,
implanted with his seed,
soul-seed of creation and salvation,
creativity and re-creation.
So it continues day and night,
The living word
bringing order out of chaos,
Day in day out,
Week in week out,
Resting from work,
working from rest,
Until the last minute of the last day,
When finally the hands of time
tip over into eternity
When all creation
bows before its Creator
And once more the Creator says
It is good...

Another piece written originally for the 10th Anniversary of New Irish Arts. There is a line in it that owes more than a little to the late great Humphrey Lyttleton on 'I'm Sorry I Haven't a Clue', which speaks volumes to my lack of real poetic pretensions!

Listening to the Word

Too many words,
drowning out the incarnate Word
That enters the world in silence
In stillness.
Background hubbub
of business that just will not wait;
The buzz of silenced phones
demanding attention.

Be still
Be still and know
Be still and know that I am
Be still and know that I am God

Shhh!
Don't speak – listen
Don't do - be

An Older Song

From Lost in Wonder, Love and Praise

Sing a new song, the Psalmist says
        Yet all songs, old and new
        Are all shaped by an older song,
        THE song;
        song of all songs;

The song of a lady for her lover;
        The Lord for his beloved.

A song which began before creation;
        A love song calling light into being,

A song breathing life into clay
A song which gave us liberty,
Yet pursued us when we wandered.
        I have loved you with an everlasting love.
        I have been eternally faithful to you.

O, if only I could say the same.
Yet I've not loved you as I should;
I have not lived the life I could.
I've sought out the shadows
Rather than living in your light.
Yet still you love me? Why?
        I am love.
        No more.
        No less.
        And you were created
        To be loved and to love.

But love turned to lust, for
luscious fresh fruit
For knowledge, or for flesh,
For riches, or for power,
For fresh tasting morsels to devour.
Love became lust;
Lust became lechery;
Liberty became license;
License became lawlessness.

    In my love I wrote to you...
I was too busy to respond...

    In my love I sang to you...
You weren't singing my tune...

    In my love I sent my son to you...
Our Son...
    Son of Woman
Son of God.
    Light in place of darkness.
    Life in place of death.

Yet in our liberty we made our choice.
Death in place of life...
Darkness in place of light...
    My Son, My Son, my one and only Son.
    Sent so that you should not be lost
    But might be set at liberty.

  Even me?
    Even you.
    Believe me... And live...
    Believe me... and love...
    Live in my love...

Love, as I love you...
Love, my beloved...
Love one another;
Love those who love you;
Love those who hate you;
Love the loveless;
Love the unlovely.
Love...

How?
    Love...

And this is love -
Not that I loved him,
But he loved me.
Loved me...
Loves me...
And always will love me...
Loved me into life...
Filled my life with love,
Filled to overflowing...
A love that brings light;
A love more constant than the sun.
A love that brings life;
A love that is stronger than death.
A love that brings liberty;
Yet a love that will not let me go...
A love without limit...
A love like no other
that I want others to know...
I am my beloved's
And he is mine...
The big day is coming...
    And everyone is invited
    Come home with me...

I go with my lover...
The tables are ready and waiting
and over the door is a banner saying
    'I love you!'

A time for singing songs...
Old songs and new songs
Come, step into the spotlight of his love
and sing a song forever old,
forever new
of light and life
of liberty and love.

I originally wrote this as a performance poem for 2 voices, male and female, for 'Lost in Wonder, Love and Praise' an event in May 2007 run by the Down District of the Methodist Church in Ireland, staged at the Waterfront in Belfast, celebrating the Life and Work of Charles Wesley, born 300 years previously. It is based on numerous passages of scripture, especially the Song of Songs and the First Letter of John.

Jonah's Story, Jonah's God

From Holden 2019

The Word of the LORD came to Jonah.
The capital L.O.R.D. Lord.
The God who is
Rather than the God we might prefer.

The Word which commanded light to be
Begins this story and all stories
That ever were
And all that are still to be written.

But will we respond to this command
Or will we just like Jonah resist?
No way Yahweh!
My story is never going there.

Is God prompting us to cross borders
And the boundaries between us and them?
Love the other
Whosoever that other might be.

Does God need to catch our attention
With sea monsters and swift growing vines
To turn us round
And reset our stories back on track?

Are we ready to change direction?
Not just to confess all our failings
But change our ways
And minds, knowing that God can change his.

Or do we prefer immutable
Kings and Gods who command and control?
Do this! Go there!
Say this, think this and don't do this!

Rather than the Word which asks questions
Wanting us to use our God given brains
And who doesn't
Finish the story...

'Jonah's Story: Jonah's God' came out of a series of lectures on the story of Jonah and the importance of story in scripture for shaping our stories. It is a short poetic distillation of some of it. Some reading it for the first time predictably objected to the idea of a God who changes his/her mind. Those of that mindset I would encourage to read the Jonah chapter 3 before coming back to me.

Wakey, Wakey

A Poem for the First Sunday of Advent

Wakey, wakey
Rise and shine.
It's Advent
The season of coming to...
Him coming to us...
Us coming to him.
Getting ready for the big day.
The time of remembering what is yet to come
And preparing for what has already arrived.
Eternity breaking into time.
Watch out...
Time ticks by
To that point when it shall be no more.
Only seconds to midnight...
Trim your wicks, not just the tree,
So you might see.
Just you wait.

A poem for the beginning of Advent written in 2008 and based on the lectionary reading from the Gospel for that week, the parable of the Wise Bridesmaids in Matthew 25.

Crying in the Wilderness

After Isaiah, John the Baptist and Janet Lees

There's still a lot of crying in the wilderness,
In the post-industrial wastelands,
The housing estates once lauded
As places of new hope.
The slums had been levelled
And the high rises raised up.
Peace had come and prosperity
Would follow in its wake.

But the hope has now run out,
The jobs have been exported,
And peace brings little prosperity
To those who always pay
the highest price for conflict.
The streets need straightened up,
The potholes need filled in
and the pavements re-laid.

Who will cry out with comfort for the hurting?
Who will call out the purveyors of pain?
Topple the towering monuments to division
And use the rubble as the foundation
for God's new motorway
straight into the hurting heart of this city,
into the heart of the problem,
into your heart and mine.

This is based on Isaiah 40: 3-11 and was originally inspired by a Janet Lees poem that Christian Aid published years ago. My version has gone through a number of revisions since then, making it more relevant to the particular city in which I have spent most of my ministry, and I am not sure how much might be directly attributable to her.

Bend and break the proud and the powerful,
Raise up those who are bent and burdened,
Lift up their eyes from all they have known
The painful past and present impotence
So that they can see that God is coming,
Bringing real peace, tangible hope
and justice that cannot be bought.

Cry out...

Isaiah's Mountain

Or The House on the Hill

Come, let us go up to the house on the hill,
The place of peace that we were promised.
The place where laws are laid down,
Where people come from all the nations
To see how peace is made.
Where guns and minds have been decommissioned
Now that the war is over.

Where the terrorist sits
With those who refused to be terrorised;
Where the innocent victim sits
With those who know that no-one is innocent;
The fearful with the fear-filled,
The gracious with the graceless,
The hopeless with the useless;
Where children play
Within walking distance
Of a nest of vipers.

Another piece inspired by the prophecy of Isaiah, this time chapters 2 and 11 and written in the wake of the collapse of the Northern Ireland's Assembly in January 2017, due to the catastrophic financial mismanagement of a renewable energy scheme and accusations of bad faith and intransigence. The meeting place of that Assembly, Parliament Buildings at Stormont, sometimes referred to as 'The House on the Hill', was the venue for the signing of the Good Friday/Belfast Peace Agreement – an agreement marked by the fact that we cannot even agree on what it is called – an omen of what was to come from it. In the wake of that agreement people have flocked to Stormont and Northern Ireland in general to hear about and learn from our 'peace process' and money has flooded in to the country from all corners of the globe to help rebuild our society and infrastructure. Sadly the Assembly that has met spasmodically in Stormont since then has demonstrated little by way of leadership in terms of building a peaceful province.

They will not harm nor destroy
At least not deliberately
We hope...

The land was once awash with money
Pouring in from foreign fields.
We've now come to the end of the treasure-trove
Yet we act like we have money to burn.
But a day is coming when,
The arrogant will be humbled
And the proud and lofty
Will be brought low.

Can't come soon enough...

Kingdom Characteristics

A kingdom of accusation and blame,
Of guilt and of shame...

An empire of acquisition and consumption,
Of fraud and corruption...

A principality of pride and presumption,
Of hubris and humiliation...

Shadows and shifting sands,
Darkness and dryness,
Deception and disappointment,
Disease, death and decay.

A kingdom constructed
   from the corpses of the powerless.
An empire erected
   on the gravestones of the poor.
A principality without principles,
Without compassion,
Without grace.

A kingdom defined by who's in and who's out.
An empire defended by force of arms.
A principality of oppression.
What we want we'll take.
What we have we'll hold.

That kingdom will crumble.
That empire will be erased.
That principality will cease.
With the coming of the Prince of Peace.

Ponder

From Luke 2: 1-20

Sssh... Stop...
Focus in...
From the affairs
Of Princes, Presidents
Prime ministers and other potentates,
On earth and in heaven.
Don't get carried away
With the excitable shepherds.
Just stop...
And ponder...

Born of water and blood

An Advent Poem

He's coming Joseph
He's coming...
The waters break...
And the agony begins.

> Through the water
> The people were saved.
> Through time of trial
> A place of promise was reached.

Wait, my love...
Wait, don't push...
The time is not right,
But he is coming...

> Why must we wait?
> Why not now?
> Let's take what is ours.
> It's the way of the world.

He's coming, my love...
Born in blood...
He is born, he breathes,
And he cries...

An Advent/Christmas poem, written in a dark period on November 30th 2010, in part prompted by my abiding detestation of the tweeness of 'Away in a Manger.'

So many tears and so much blood.
The blood of battlefields
And the blood of beasts
Flowing free in the temple.

Born of water and blood
Born to bleed and die
Born to cleanse and restore
Born that we might live...

Born of water and blood.

Bethl'em Road

A Song for Christmas

Down Bethl'em road from Nazareth,
Came Joseph and his wife,
Within her womb God's promise bloomed,
His Word, the Light of Life.
He came to take on flesh and blood,
To show us all the way,
And through the night a star so bright,
Hailed the dawning of his day.

And on the hills round Bethlehem,
Some shepherds heard the song,
The angels sing of a new born King
Awaited for so long.
They find him midst the filth and grime,
In a bed of straw and hay,
Ignored by the earth that he brought to birth,
The Lord Almighty lay.

And from the east to Bethlehem
Come men who saw the sign.
These eastern seers travelled two long years
To present their gifts so fine.
Gold they did bring, fit for a king
And a scent of untold worth.
But the gift of myrrh that they offer third
Spoke of death and not of birth.

From Bethlehem his parents fly
To save their son from harm,
But others die and mothers cry
And wail in their alarm.

The powers that be had come to see
That child as a source of strife.
His birth meant despair to the people there
But his coming brought us life.

From Bethlehem to Jerusalem
Is not so very far.
Thirty-three years on, on a cold spring dawn
He died on a wooden spar.
From he first drew breath 'til his cruel death
For him there was no room,
He took the blame for our sin and shame
And was laid in a borrowed tomb.

But on our streets and roads today,
The Lord can still be found,
Wherever we will bend the knee
The angels' song resounds.
To heaven raise God's glorious praise
And on the earth be peace,
Where once again Christ comes to reign
His grace will never cease.

I've used it this couple of times in worship around Christmas, so it actually does work. The tune is 'Raglan Road...' and both the tune and form of the original song shaped this.

The Work of Christmas – Continued

After Howard Thurman and Michael Dougherty

When the angel choir has gone home to heaven,
When the last notes of their song have faded,
When the shepherds are back to watching their sheep,
And Bethlehem is no longer so busy,
When all those gathered for the census have gone home,
When the magi are making their way back east,
When the special star has long gone from the sky,
That is when the work of Christmas begins:
> To seek the lost,
> To heal the broken,
> To comfort the sorrowing,
> To feed the hungry,
> To release the oppressed,
> To bring glory to God,
> To bring peace on earth,
> To be a light to the nations.

When the carollers have stopped all their singing,
When the TV schedules are back to normal,
When all family and friends have gone back home,
When the decorations are all dismantled,

I had never before come across the piece entitled 'The Work of Christmas' until December 2018, when I was chasing up the origins of a Facebook meme. It turned out to be a reworking of a poem, also known as 'When the Song of the Angels is Stilled' originally written by Howard Thurman an African-American author, philosopher, theologian, educator, and civil rights leader, but adapted by Michael Dougherty, Co-Chair of the Social Justice Committee at Sacred Heart Cathedral in Whitehorse, Yukon. The original has been used as the basis for a choral carol which seems to be very popular in America, but which, despite its subject and sentiment, leaves me cold. But it did serve as the building blocks for this 2-verse adaptation.

When the star-topped tree is packed away again,
When we are all back working hard at our desks,
That is when the work of Christmas begins:
> To welcome the refugee,
> To heal a broken world,
> To work that none should hunger,
> To break down walls,
> To renew the nations,
> To pursue justice for all,
> To sing a song of hope.

Not So Good News

Christmas 2016

A year of untruth
And dis-grace.
A year of grieving for the famous
And a year of infamy;
Of public grief, but little else
For the poor and the powerless,
The vulnerable victims
Crushed between a callous dictator
   and ruthless rebels
Both backed by chess-playing super-powers
Dealing death by remote control.
Another year of mass migration
Young men fleeing fighting and hunger
Pathfinders seeking peace and hope
For their families back home,
If they still have homes, or families,
Finding their way onto posters
Promoting dread and division,
A year of stark choices
Yes, No, In, Out...
More of the same or who knows what.

A year of democracy dragged through the dirt,
Power to the people...
Lies to the people...
Contempt for the people
From those seekers after power
And those who want to hold on to it
At all costs.
A new word for the dictionary.
Brexit Means What?

More money for the NHS?
Taking back control?
Let's make America great again
By building a wall, or a fence, or a line in the sand,
By locking her up
Or giving free reign to grope her
Whoever she may be.

Another year of terror
Terrorists doing what it says on the tin
Delivering death by the truckload
And many other means,
And political parties completing their job
By spreading the fear far and wide,
Divide and be conquered by animosity and anxiety,
While the biggest threat to our existence,
And all life on this wonderful world,
Is downplayed or denied
As 'a Chinese plot' or 'Green guff',
While we burn money to heat empty sheds,
And more and more homeless sleep rough
On cold streets,
Although the streets are strangely
Unseasonably warm.

We need good news for bad
A new year for the old
Grace and truth
Needs to take on flesh again.

I originally wrote this over Christmas 2016 and revised it in the run up to Year's Eve. 2016 was a year when many famous people died, the civil war in Syria rumbled on, refugees poured into Europe, fuelling increased xenophobia and influencing what was a pivotal year politically in Northern Ireland, the UK and USA. For some of us it did not seem to be a pivot in the right direction. Time will tell...

Epiphany Gifts

Gold.
Suitable for a King.
But probably one like Herod,
Or an Emperor like Augustine,
Not the King born in Bethlehem
And crowned in Jerusalem
With thorns.

Frankincense.
Aromatic Arabian resin
Might sweeten the smell of a stable
Or enhance the smell of a sacrifice
Offered up by the priesthood,
To ameliorate the bloodlust
Of their god.

Myrrh.
Another Arabian resin;
A scent associated with temple worship,
Not a stable or a carpenter's workshop;
Used to anoint kings, anaesthetise pain,
And cover up the stench of death.
So suitable.

Today.
What would resonate?
Something technological or pharmaceutical?
Something representing power or piety?
A gun or sacred text, or even better, both?
Would our gifts mark us out
As wise?

Outside is the Garden

After Matthew 6: 25-27

Outside is the garden
with birds on the wing
and trees coming into leaf,
offering healing for the soul.

Outside is the garden
beyond two panes of glass,
observed but not experienced,
watched but not walked in.

Outside is the garden
and no sword-wielding angel
stands barring the way
to this small suburban Eden.

Outside is the garden
but you toil on, brow furrowed
ploughing through paperwork
in self-imposed exile.

Outside is the garden
but inside your central-heated
double-glazed bubble
thorns and thistles throttle green shoots.

Outside, the garden…

Companions on a Journey

From Connexions on a Journey

Some people don't like travelling on public transport
Beside other people; smelly people;
Rude people; poor people;
Noisy people; nosy people;
Young people; old people;
Some people don't like people...
They prefer cars...
Jesus likes people...
People like you and me;
People not like you and me;
People not liked by you and me;
People who don't like you and me;
People who don't know you and me;
But Jesus knows them
And he knows you and me
And despite all that he knows
He invites us all to join him on his journey.
I think Jesus would have liked public transport.

'Companions on a Journey' was written for the 'Connexions on a Journey' event during the Methodist Church in Ireland Conference at St Patrick's College, Drumcondra, Dublin in 2004.

The Fig Tree

From Luke 13: 1-9

A landowner had a fig-tree,
planted in his vineyard,
and he went to look for fruit on it,
but did not find any.
So he said to the gardener
who took care of the vineyard:

> 'For the past three years
> I've been looking for fruit from this tree
> but haven't found any.
> So cut it down!
> Why should I waste soil on it?'

> But the gardener said:
> 'Sir, leave it alone for one more year,
> and I'll dig round it and fertilise it.
> If it bears fruit next year, fine!
> If not, then cut it down.'

The religious leaders,
the priests and the Pharisees,
kept an eye on the storyteller
to see what fruit
his teaching would produce.
But they saw nothing good
and so said to themselves:

> 'For three years now
> we've watched this country rabbi
> but have found nothing good in him.
> We need to cut him down
> before he poisons
> all the people.'

The champions of the people,
the zealots and their like,
kept an eye out
for the coming of the Messiah,
but they saw no-one suitable
and so they said to themselves:

> 'For many long years now
> we've been watching and waiting
> but things never change for the better.
> We need to cut ourselves free!
> Drive the Romans from our soil.'

Young firebrands of the Church,
in every generation,
keep looking for signs
of growth and fruitfulness,
but are sadly disappointed
and so they say to themselves:

> 'For many years now
> we've been (im)patiently waiting
> but things never change for the better.
> We need to cut ourselves free
> from those tired old structures
> and start again in fresh fields.'

The upright members of the Church,
in every generation,
keep looking for signs of repentance
in those all around them.
But they are sadly disappointed
and so they say to themselves:

> 'For many years now
> we've bent over backwards
> but haven't seen any change
> in their behaviour or beliefs.
> We should give up on them
> brush the dust off our feet.'

>> But the gardener said:
>> 'Sir, leave it alone for one more year,
>> and I'll dig round it and fertilise it.
>> If it bears fruit next year, fine!
>> If not, then cut it down.'

One more year...

Thanks go to Mark Sweeney for setting my thoughts in motion on this poetic reflection on Jesus' parable of the Fig Tree.

I Love You

You're Welcome

Simon Peter,
There's no denying it,
I love you.
Do you love me?
Come on,
Follow me, and love others
As I have loved you.

Judas,
Purse-bearer, guilt-bearer,
You did what you thought needed done,
For whatever reason.
But I love you.
So come on,
Give me a kiss.

Pilate,
The truth is,
I love you too
And all those in positions of power,
Fearful of those above and below.
So let me wash not just your hands
But your heart.

Caiaphas,
It is better that one man die
For the sake of the people,
Is it?
I love you too,

Though the word seems absent
From the lexicon of your religion.

Mary,
The first to see me but not the last,
And sadly not the first nor the last woman
to have been maligned by men of faith.
Oh how I love you.
Let me dry your tears.
Now we can embrace.

It's strange what cocktails of things prompt the things that I write. They are, as the title of this anthology suggests, frequently just word doodles. The following short reflections written in May 2019 were stirred up not only by preaching on Jesus' dealing with Simon Peter in John 20 the previous week, but also reading stories of politicians that I would bitterly disagree with, a response by a colleague to a comment I had made about a political commentator that I dislike, seeing a church notice board on my way into work that says 'All Welcome' when I don't actually think that all would be welcome in that particular church, except on their terms, and listening to the gospel song 'People Get Ready' on my car playlist on the same journey, and specifically the verse that says

> *'There ain't no room*
> *For the hopeless sinner*
> *Who would hurt all mankind*
> *Just to save his own.'*

And from that stew came this...You're welcome...

Through My Eyes

A Song

Can you see things through my eyes?
The childless woman cries.
The years of trying, probing, prying...
While across the street a girl is crying
With three wee children by three different men
And not a penny from any of them.
Can you see things through my eyes?

Can you see things through my eyes?
The jobless father cries.
Thrown on the scrap heap at forty seven
Don't tell me there's a good God in heaven.
I'm living off pills, we've mountains of bills,
And my son is always in trouble.
Can you see things through my eyes?

> *Through my eyes*
> *My tear washed eyes*
> *You can see things much clearer*
> *Through my eyes.*

Can you see things through my eyes?
The hopeless young man cries.
No qualifications, no expectations.
No job, no hobbies and no ambitions.
The only hope for me and mine

This was specifically as a song for Diane Petherick (now Holt) as a fund-raiser for The Link Family and Community Centre, Newtownards. It was then adapted and recorded on the CD 'Through My Eyes' with music by Darren Baird.

Is to leave this rotten world behind.
Can you see things through my eyes?

Can you see things through my eyes?
The bereaved mother cries.
Tell me who's to blame? Who counts the cost?
Who knows the future that's been lost?
No-one dares tell me why my baby died.
Everyone tells me comforting lies.
Can you see things through my eyes?

> *Through my eyes*
> *My tear washed eyes*
> *You can see things much clearer*
> *Through my eyes.*

Can you see things through my eyes?
Our loving saviour cries...
Do you see the pain, the struggle the loss,
Or do you see the fault, the sin, the cost?
Do you see those who deserve your help
Or those who get what they deserve,
Or do you see things through my eyes?

> *Through my eyes*
> *My tear washed eyes*
> *You can see things much clearer*
> *Through my eyes.*

Through your hands...
I can reach out in love
Through your hands.

> *Through my eyes*
> *My tear washed eyes*
> *You can see things much clearer*
> *Through my eyes.*

The Theatre of God's Glory

After John Calvin

The theatre of God's glory...
A stage lit by the sun, the moon, and myriad stars...
An ever changing backdrop of sky and land and sea...
A cast of untold billions,
Yet each one known intimately by the director
Who urges all to play their part to the full,
Directing every step... watching over every word...
Intricately weaving everyone into a beautiful ballet...
Accompanied not by music from the pit,
But from above and beyond.
The drama played out on that stage
Far surpasses anything that even Shakespeare could write,
Never mind an infinite number of chimpanzees
Bashing away on an infinite number of typewriters.
Such a script is not the product of statistical happenstance
But the inspired improvisation of the author and director
Of all.
In a drama of life and death
Of new life and infinite opportunities
The tragedy of good gone bad...
The comedy of creator become creature
A true theatre of the absurd...
The first act has ended
The curtain of death has fallen and Christ has risen.
But the performance continues...
Prompted by the Spirit
Until, at last, the final curtain falls
And the applause of heaven rings out.

Another piece written originally for the 10th Anniversary of New Irish Arts, inspired by John Calvin's titular description of creation as 'the theatre of God's glory' but also drawing on my own theatrical pretentions.

Sea and Star

You're the sea on which I sail:
      Uncharted and unfathomable,
      Unpredictable and incomparable.
You're the stars by which I steer:
      By day blazing your way,
      Across the arc of the azure sky,
      By night the pin pricks of light,
      That puncture the darkness.
You're the wind that drives me on:
      Beyond the horizon of my understanding,
      From which there can be no returning.
And when my journey is done
You're the safe harbour
Where, finally, I can drop anchor...

Written in the dark on the back of a beer mat in the Black Box, Belfast, after a Karine Polwart gig in 2010, when she sang the song 'Terminal Star' and told a story about a vintage boat on one of the Scottish Lochs. Karine Polwart is an artist who both inspires me to write and makes me realise the limits of my skills.

A Feather on the Breath of God

After Hildegard of Bingen

Holy Spirit:
The life of all creatures;
The cause of all movement;
The source of all song.
You are the breath – bring us life.
You are the salve – soothe our souls.
You are the balm – heal our wounds.
You are the fire – warm our hearts.
You are the wisdom – open our minds.
You are the light – guide our feet.

The German Benedictine nun, Hildegard of Bingen (1098 – 1179), was a veritable renaissance woman, long before the Renaissance. She was an abbess, poet, composer (she even had a hit album recently), theologian, philosopher and mystic, is considered to be the founder of scientific natural history in Germany, writing influential botanical and medicinal texts, was the author of what is possibly the earliest German liturgical drama, arguably the oldest surviving morality play, and inventor of a constructed language known as Lingua Ignota. She might easily be seen as a patron saint of the modern environmental movement with her strong sense of the wholeness of creation. Given her range of interests she has always intrigued me, especially given that she had a strong sense of how they were all integrated.

> *'Underneath all the texts, all the sacred psalms and canticles, these watery varieties of sounds and silences, terrifying, mysterious, whirling and sometimes gestating and gentle must somehow be felt in the pulse, ebb, and flow of the music that sings in me. My new song must float like a feather on the breath of God.'*

This is my version of her prayer which occurs in a number of variants in different sources and in different places in her writings. One day with a suitable dictionary in hand I might seek out the original.

Frankie's Prayer

A version of a famous Franciscan Prayer

Lord, make me a wellspring
of your all-pervading peace.
Where there is hatred and fear,
let me show and sow love;
Where there is injury and hurt,
let me bring healing and forgiveness;
Where there is doubt and despair,
let me bring faith and hope;
Where there is darkness,
let your light shine through me;
And where there is sadness,
may I share your sustaining joy.

My God and Master,
shift my focus from myself.
May I seek to comfort others
rather than remain comfortable;
May I listen and hear,
rather than seek to speak;
May I love indiscriminately
rather than seek love selfishly.
For its only when we give away
that we have room to receive;
It is in forgiving
that we find ourselves forgiven;
And it is in dying
that we can really begin
to live life to the full.

In like vein to my re-writing of St Hildegard's prayer, this is my take on what is often, erroneously described as the Prayer of St Francis of Assisi, when it actually seems to have originated no earlier than the beginning of the 20th Century, although it was in a Franciscan publication and is very much in the spirit of St Francis.

Beyond the Grey Sky

After St Francis of Assisi's Canticle of Creation

Beyond the grey sky
sits Brother Sun,
but his heat drives Brother Wind
and draws the waters
into clouds.

Those clouds, our sisters,
that shield the sun
bear the water, sustaining water,
to the parched earth;
Mother Earth.

From earth we came;
to earth we return,
but all through our lives
we are watched over
by you, our Father God;
unseen, all seeing.

Grey sky may loom over us
but Brother Sun shines on,
and your love for us
is more constant than that sun,
with no beginning and no ending.
Praise you.

A prayer that can more reliably be attributed to St Francis of Assisi, is his 'Canticle of Creation/the Sun' and this is a meditation based on that.

I Believe

I believe,
not in a creed,
not in a list,
but in a life,
a story,
a story that changes
other stories,
other lives...
my life –
not at a point in the past,
but every day
a presence in the present.
I believe
in love.
I believe
I'm loved.
I believe
I'm called to love.
I believe
even in the midst
of my unbelief.

The Dawning of the Day

From Genesis: A Celebration of Creativity

I'm grown up now...
but I'm still afraid of the dark...
I pretend that I'm not...
But then adults are good at pretending...
Children play 'let's pretend'
but they're only practicing
for the serious pretending
that goes on in adulthood...
Pretending that we're happy...
Pretending that we're confident...
Pretending that we like each other...
Pretending that we like ourselves...
I pretend that I'm not afraid of the dark...
But I am...

I'm afraid of what hides in the shadows...
Murderers and maniacs and monsters...
And memories...
Memories of things I've done and not done...
Memories of things done to me...
Dark things...
That I pretend never happened...
But they did...
And in the dark I see them...
Black on black...
Ready to engulf me...
To snuff out the light of my life...

But before I drown in the darkness,
I have learned to look for the light...
And it is always there...

Somewhere...
at the flick of a switch,
or by opening a door,
or peering into the night sky,
to see a star...
A small speck shining
across the almost infinite reaches of space...
A light that began its journey
millions of years before I was born...
before my fears began...
Echo of a light created by God's word
to banish the darkness...
The dawning of the day...

This started life as a monologue inspired by Genesis 1: 3-5 and John 1: 5, and I supposed it still is, just re-formatted as free-form blank verse. It, like some of the poems earlier in this collection, originated as part of New Irish Art's 10th Anniversary presentation based on Genesis 1 and billed as 'A Celebration of Creativity.'

A Trinitarian Creed

We believe in one God,
A Community of Three in a Unity of Being.

We believe in the Creator,
Creator of sky, earth and sea,
Creator of birds, animals and fish,
And us...
Creator of all that is, seen, unseen and unimaginable.

We believe in Jesus Christ,
Born of God...
Born of woman...
Born, lived, died, and rose again,
Born to teach, save, and give us hope.

We believe in the Holy Spirit,
The all-pervading breath of God,
Who breathed life into us in the beginning,
Who breathed life into the Church at Pentecost,
Who brings gifts and strength and encouragement.

We believe in God, the Three in One.
The One in Three
The blessed, sacred Trinity.
An eternal dance of personality;
Diversity in unity;
Creator, redeemer, sustainer.

We believe in the Church;
Diversity in unity;
A community stretching around the globe

And through the ages,
And stretching out to all creation
Redeeming, sustaining.

We believe in God.
We live in God.
Three in One, One in Three.
The living, loving Trinity.

Poetry and Prayer

October 2013

Meeting for worship and prayer with Friends,
Silently sitting in a prayer room,
A cell or silo, cut through with a single window
Through which, at just the right angle
One can see the world go by...
One can see the world go buy.

Silence suffused by the constant rumble of traffic.
Pierced by a wailing alarm crying wolf,
And punctuated by prompted words,
Through which, in the right light,
One can see a wider world...
One can see a wiser world.

Worship is not a matter of words and music,
And prayer is not retreat from the world,
But an active interweaving of heaven and earth,
Through which, in the right time,
One can see another world...
One can see in another world.

This was prompted by a shared meeting of Belfast South Methodist and South Belfast Society of Friends at the Agape Centre Prayer Room in October 2013 on the eve of national poetry day. The Agape Centre is on the Lisburn Road, one of the busiest arterial roads in Belfast with a thriving shopping and coffee culture.

Guilt and Gratitude

I carry guilt and gratitude
In roughly equal measure,
But both merely background noise
While I get on with my life.

Guilt when reading about the poor
Or watch wars waged on TV.
Gratitude when I consider
My prosperity and peace.

Guilt when I hear of the struggles
Of older generations.
Gratitude when I consider
My comparative cushiness.

Guilt because of the legacy
We are leaving to our children.
Gratitude when I consider
The world into which I was born.

Guilt when I speak to the victims
Of our recent local conflicts.
Gratitude when I consider
How miles and schooling kept me safe.

Guilt and gratitude
Pointless if periodic,
Prompting swift, if heartfelt, prayers,
Yet making no difference
To a life lived now
And in the future.

Dust on the breeze

Musings on Mortality

Dust on the breeze,
Is that what life comes to?

A hilltop offers fresh perspectives,
New insights on how things are
Down below.
But is that the revelation
In the cold light of dawn
And the chilling wind
Of a mountaintop?

Are we a random assortment of elements
Briefly bound together
In an animated form?

From dust you came
And to dust you shall return -
Nothing more.

But what of the years in between?
The love, the laughter,
The anger, the tears,
Hopes and dreams and memories
And faith?

A piece written after conducting a service where the ashes of a member of my congregation were scattered to the winds from the top of a local hill at dawn.

Are they little more than
Dust on the breeze?
Motes momentarily catching the light
On the updraft?

But the light is the light of the rising sun.
A dawning day and a coming kingdom
A sure and certain
Hope...

The Fixer

When the fixer cannot fix it,
When the coper cannot cope,
When the purveyor of hope,
Has nothing left for himself.

When every day brings more heartache,
When each night brings more despair,
When the world seems so unfair,
And darkness is triumphant,

When the storm sends you spiralling,
When the earth quakes beneath your feet,
When enemies plot your defeat,
And others sigh at your demise.

When you are way beyond your depth,
When the going is worse than tough,
When mere words are not enough,
What you need is incarnation.

The uncalled for call,
The unasked for gift,
The present of presence,
The slightest spark of light,
The embrace of everlasting arms,
Made flesh in a friend.

Domestic Drama

The age old drama
Of predator and prey
Played out in a suburban garden;
Death crouching in the flowerbed,
Garlanded with yellow blossoms.
Narrowed eyes darting,
Watching for flitting quarry.
An Egyptian goddess observing
The fall of every sparrow, and robin,
As assiduously as our heavenly Father.
Ears flicking, muscles coiled;
Finally unleashed
In a blurred flurry of fur,
Frustrated by a lack of wings.

Regathering her dignity
The huntress returns
Settling for dried pellets,
Rather than fresh feathered flesh,
Then settling down
On a human servant's lap
To be petted and purr,
Peaceful innocence restored.

Aerial Battle

A haiku

Buzzard harried by
Two very angry song birds.
Togetherness wins.

A piece written after conducting a service where the ashes of a member of my congregation were scattered to the winds from the top of a local hill at dawn.

Wagtail

Dromantine October 2019

Wagtail walking the ridge tile
Stark against the skyline
Only one direction possible
Until
They take flight

Another short poem inspired by birds, this time coming out of watching a pied wagtail that was a repeated visitor to a rooftop outside the window of a room at Dromantine Retreat Centre where I was reflecting on some seemingly binary decisions I had to make. Sometimes we just need to consider things from another angle.

For Claudia

Ten years on

A small cat purring
Mysteriously keeps the
Big black dog at bay.

And yet another attempt at a haiku. This, and the subsequent piece is inspired by my cat, Claudia, named after CJ in the West Wing. She joined our family in 2010 while I was in the midst of a prolonged bout of depression. We had 'lost' our previous cat earlier in the year and had vowed not to get another but an American friend 'bullied us' into getting Claudia from the Assisi Animal Sanctuary because it would 'do me good'. And she did. And 10 years on she still does.

Protestare

For not Against

I'm Protestant...
I'm also pro-Catholic.
Pro-Unionist and pro-Republican.
Pro-Irish and pro-British.
Pro-Israeli and pro-Palestinian.
Pro-Ukrainian and pro-Russian.
Pro-American and pro-European.
Pro-Scottish and pro-English.
Pro-People.

Anti-violence
Anti-injustice
Anti-inequality
Anti-oppression
Anti-division
Anti-simplistic oppositional politics
Divide and conquer
Us and ours
Them and theirs
A long record of wrongs
Zero sum
They win
We lose.

On social media I am regularly asked to sign different petitions, attend different protest events and encouraged to share different articles about various contentious situations. I am very cautious about doing so coming from Northern Ireland where every global disagreement becomes viewed through the myopic green and orange tinted lenses worn by the people in this place, leading most discussions on social media to become relatively predictable in terms of who supports what or whom. So, I have tended to keep well clear… But the above piece expresses some of my frustrations, and also some of the basic principles that guide my thoughts in responding to conflicts here and abroad.

My enemy's enemy is my friend,
But I long to make my enemy my friend,
And to make erstwhile enemies
into newfound friends.

And where I cannot find a way
of doing that directly,
I will pray for those
who risk their lives
to bring love and peace
to places of hatred and conflict.

Palestine... Israel...
Iraq... Syria...
India... Pakistan
Northern Ireland...

I am Protestant.

That Kingdom

That Kingdom you taught us to pray for
Heaven come to earth
It's your Kingdom – not ours
Your power – not ours
Your glory – not ours
Let it be so
An overturning of the status quo

Lustily and With Good Courage

A Methodist Haiku

Being born in song
May I still sing out boldly
Under death's shadow

The title for this comes from John Wesley's instructions on hymn-singing while the first line is from the first line of the 1933 Methodist Hymnbook. It was inspired by a funeral and two friends in ministry and their families going through a heart-breaking journey.

Joy

Joy
in music
in the virtuosity of a guitarist
and the emotive power of a choir

in science
in the intricacy of genetics
and the vast scope of cosmology

in sport
in the precision of a golf putt
and the raw strength of a rugby scrum

in conversation
in catching up with a dear friend
and a casual encounter with a stranger

in words
in a funny turn of phrase
and a carefully crafted argument

in the post
in a generous and unexpected gift
and a heart laid bare in gratefulness

in sunshine
and in shadow
on the wing
or perching lightly
but if it falls within your grasp
don't hold it too tight...
let it fly on
to brighten another's day.

Homeless

Portland 2019

Sleep in the daytime
Beneath the view of passers-by:
Priest, pastor, layperson and typically
Uncaring contemporary Samaritan.
Sleep, because night-time is coming.

Sleep in the summer
Spoiling the streets for foreigners
Clutching guidebooks and mobile phones
Seeking but ignoring the real city.
Sleep, because winter is coming.

Sleep away the hunger.
Walk away the cold.
Self-medicate the voices
And the pain away.

Condemned for your choices
When the choices of others
Have condemned you to a kerbside,
Have robbed you of a roof,
Health,
Dignity,
Humanity.

Prompted by my first visit to the Pacific NW of the USA in July 2019 and the shock level of homelessness I encountered in Portland and Seattle, where it is a feature of every street in both city centres. It is also increasing in my home city of Belfast, in Northern Ireland, but it is exacerbated in the US by the lack of affordable/appropriate social housing, and health care costs, especially for mental health issues, addiction and, soberingly, given my own health condition, diabetes.

Where is the humanity
That allows such indignity?
Your worldly possessions
Crammed into a shopping cart
Designed for people to take home
More than they need.
While what you need
Is somewhere to call home.

Where do Poems Grow?

With thanks to Barbara Kingsolver

Where do poems grow?
On the periphery of vision,
Evading direct attention.
A distraction en route
   to somewhere important.

A deer dashing across a field;
A flash of a kingfisher's wing;
A Perseid streak in the night sky;
An overheard phrase
   across a crowded room.

Not often crafted, but birthed
Like Athena, fully armed
Out of an overfull head.
In the furrows of the mind
   between the cash crops.

Inspired by some words by Barbara Kingsolver, the novelist, essayist and poet in her anthology of essays 'Small Wonder': 'I rarely think of poetry as something I make happen; it is more accurate to say that it happens to me... I've overheard poems, virtually complete, in elevators or restaurants where I was minding my own business... When a poem does arrive, I gasp as if an apple had fallen into my hand, and give thanks for the luck involved. Poems are everywhere but easy to miss. I know I might very well stand under that tree all day, whistling, looking off to the side, waiting for a red delicious poem to fall so I could own it forever. But like as not, it wouldn't. Instead it will fall right when I'm changing the baby, or breaking up a rodeo event involving my children and the dog, or wiping my teary eyes while I'm chopping onions and listening to the news; then that apple will land with a thud and will roll under the bed with the dust bunnies and lie there forgotten and lost for all time. There are dusty, lost poems all over my house, I assure you. In yours, too, I'd be willing to bet.'

Found, unlooked for,
When searching under clutter,
For something else.
Wedged between books,
Mouldering at the back of the fridge
   or stuck down the back of the settee
   with £3.76, a button and a pen.

Carefully Chosen Words

With thanks to Brian Bilston

Classical allusions
Providing cover for
Unalloyed callousness.
Costly educations
Affording a wealthy
Vocabulary with
Which to sneer and mock.
An armoury of wit
Without warmth or wisdom,
Considered yet with no
Consideration as
To the price paid
By others for their ill
Chosen words: sound bites
That stick in the mind with
Barbs that tear the flesh and

Written in the wake of one of the most toxic evenings I have ever witnessed in the coverage of Westminster politics where insults and abuse were hurled across the chamber as Boris Johnson tried to force through his Brexit deal. It is influenced in part by a short and pithy poem by Brian Bilston on the danger of ill-chosen words, posted on social media by my previously mentioned friend Rev. Micky Youngson. She followed it up with the following pertinent verse of scripture: 'Take note of this: everyone should be quick to listen, slow to speak and slow to become angry' (James 1: 19).

My own piece had been percolating in my mind over a number of days and weeks, with references to classical literature being dropped in to speeches to give them an educated gloss, and other crass statements being made by different people playing to their supporters with no regard for the ultimate effects of their words and policies. But it doesn't just apply to the political leaders of the UK and US, but to all those who toss out cheap jibes and soundbites... And indeed memes on social media... We can all be guilty of it... Particularly when we are angry about one thing or another... And anger certainly doesn't seem to be in short supply at the moment, particularly not with in the sphere of social media.

Spirit of those beyond
The well upholstered and
Dark wood panelled halls of
Privilege and power,
Where allies cheer and jeer
And foes seek to score cheap
Points in a game where the
Losers are all of us.

Makers

Blessed are the peace makers

Making up
Making amends
Making friends
Making time for others
Making space for possibilities
Making cups of tea
Making a fool of yourself
Making sense
Making a stand
Making a start
Making
Not destroying

Poems and Ploughshares

With thanks to Osip Mandelstam

> Swords turned into ploughshares
> Words turning over fallow fields
> Cutting into the grassy ground
> Uncovering broken treasures
> Of times almost forgotten
> Slowing the progress of the plough
> Revealing rich black undersoil
> Nourished by blood and decay
> Ready to receive the sown seed
> Wheat or weeds

In Avivah Gottlieb Zornberg's psychoanalytic, midrashic comentary 'The Murmuring Deep' she quotes Osip Mandelstam saying:

> *'poetry is the plough tearing open and turning over time so that the deep layers of it, its rich black undersoil, ends up on the surface.... Mankind ... craves, like a ploughman, for the virgin soil of time.'*

The combination of this my current parallel reading of Gladys Ganiel's 'Considering Grace', dealing with how the Presbyterian Church handled the Troubles, Robert Harris's 'The Second Sleep', which turns on the relationship between the past, future, present and faith and a book produced by my son Ciaran's archaeology department prompted this poem, in which I stole a particularly evocative line. But I freely acknowledge that artistically and intellectually, I am little more than one of those birds that swoop in after the plough or the seed drill to snatch something tasty after someone else has done the hard work.

Omphalos

A poem for New Year's Eve

What binds us to what was,
Or what is yet to be?
Is it life-giving,
Or necrotic,
Poisoning both?
There comes a time
After the agony of emergence
That the cord must be cut.
Only then can both survive
And thrive.
A scar will remain.
A memory of the unremembered,
Both nurturing and traumatic,
Too often disregarded
As a focus of selfish contemplation,
Seeing oneself as the centre of the world,
Yet actually a relic
Of dependence and devotion.

But there is no going back
Nicodemus was right in that.
A new connection
Must be made and tended.

But first, cut...

This was written in December 2019, again prompted by reading Avivah Gottlieb Zornberg's 'The Murmuring Deep' within which she looks at various midrashes on Rebekah and Rachel, against the background of a family birth, fears for the future with the New Year just on the horizon and the abiding inability to deal healthily with the past in this part of the world.

Omphalos II

A poem for the New Year

The place where two eagles meet
Past and future fighting on the wing
While down below
The profound present
Remains to be explored.

I started 2020 in a similar vein to where I left off in 2019, thinking about how we deal with the past and with fear of the future. In this I pick up on the legend concerning the location of the Omphalos (navel) at the centre of the world by Zeus. He supposedly set off twin eagles from either end of the Earth and they met over Delphi, which was the site of the mysterious oracle of Apollo. In later Christian tradition the 'omphalos' was said to be in the Church of the Holy Sepulchre in Jerusalem, a place which again has not been devoid of conflict.

Squaring the Circle

For Nuala

Look up,
In thankfulness
That we are where we are.
Look up,
In hopefulness
for the unclaimed future.
Thanksgiving and hope,
Gratitude and grace,
One feeding into the other
In an unbroken circle,
Breaking the old circle
Of hopelessness and hatred,
Unforgiveness and fear.
Look up.

In many ways this is a partner piece to 'The Ballad of the Big Fish' at the beginning of the anthology as it was written about a piece of public art a short way up river from it, as part of the 'Wonderful Wander' for 4 Corners 2020. The Beacon of Hope is a 19.5 metres high metal sculpture by Andy Scott constructed in 2007 in the recently designated 'Thanksgiving Square' on the banks of the Lagan. It has been given several nicknames including Nuala with the Hula (credited to Gerard Doyle), the Belle on the Ball, the Thing with the Ring or the Angel of Thanksgiving.

Building a City of Grace

3 Haiku

A city of grace –
Take time to imagine it
And tell its story

Build a space for grace –
A place for new perspectives
Facing the future

A grace period –
Pause to consider whether
There's a better way

These three 'urban haiku' were prompted by the 2020 4 Corners Festival which had the title as its theme. The first was prompted by Avivah Gottlieb Zornberg's commentary on the story of Ruth in her book 'The Murmuring Deep' and festival participant Damian Gorman's poem 'If I Was Us, I Wouldn't Start From Here'. The second came from the words of architect Arthur Parke at an event in Ulster University in Belfast's Cathedral Quarter, a place where there is currently an ideological battle going on regarding the built environment, heritage and cultural life, while the last came from an event called 'Grace Moments' where participants reflected on key events that changed the course of their lives?

Death of a Pastor

With thanks to Clive James

Has it come to this?
I've been in this hospital room many times,
Or if not this one, many like it.
Ministering to others.
Praying prayers that neither the dying
Nor their companions could hear
Over the din of impending death.
Reading words from a book
That many of them think
Is as dead as they soon will be.

I've had them all here.
The benefit of clergy.
The chaplain – with no collar on
Just a faux-frown married uncomfortably
To a supposedly comforting smile,
A name badge and religious language
To distinguish him from a doctor
Or a porter,
Except even the porters wear uniforms.

The young minister, recently appointed,
Who rarely visited before I ended up here,
And seems uncertain of what to say
In the presence of a pastoral fossil.
A procession of my peers,
Here to see if I will
Beat them to the finishing line;
Jockeying for position
Over who will have to pronounce
That I have run the race,
I have fought that good fight
(Sometimes with them)

And kept the faith,
Though not necessarily in that order.

There have been so many
That I know my wife would have wished
To drive them from the room,
Like Jesus cleansing the temple,
With or without a whip;
Especially when the President arrived
To bring the prayers of the whole Church,
Like a pious postman.
I don't know the man, nor he me
So why should he be a spectator
Of my sadly slow decline?
But she said nothing
Rather she graciously accepted
Each clerical intruder in turn,
Surrendering me to the Church in death
As she had often done in life.

My real friends (some of whom are clerics,
Some even Christians) and family
Have also been here constantly,
Changing the guard
According to some unwritten rota,
From the time they knew
That I wasn't walking out again,
This time...
Because there have been many
False alarms recently...
The last trump prematurely blown,
As different organs have shown signs
Of a lifetime's lack of self-care.
Until finally there was no way back.
Slipping away,
Unable to do anything for myself,
Thankfully spared the pains

Of recent years by the miracle
Of morphine.

They think that has rendered me
Unconscious,
Just because, unlike myself,
I do not respond with words.
I cannot speak,
But even if I could
What's left to say?
Words were my stock-in-trade
And I used plenty in my time.
Now I just listen.
To the inconsequentialities
Of conversation across my bed;
Football, films, food,
Relationships and rugby
People and politics...
Politics –
Not sad to be leaving that behind,
For a new regime.
A new heaven and a new earth
Where there will be no more
Death or mourning or crying or pain
Or bloody politicians.
They will have passed away
With that sea, which will be no more.

I will miss the sea.
Though of course I know that
All of that is just John's apocalyptic poetry
Although such poetry holds more reality
For me than concrete prose.
I long for a poetic paradise,
Rather than the prosaic reality,
Of catheters and cannulas,
The smell of antiseptic and decay.

I cannot speak, but I can smell
As well as hear,
And each scent conjures up
A lifetime of memories,
Good and not so good.
Oh for the scent of bacon buttie!
Although strangely, I am not hungry
For the first time in my life!

However, I thirst,
Like Christ on his cross.
I thirst,
And like those watching him die
My watchers lift a sponge on a stick
To my lips,
Soaked, not with wine
But water.
I could do with a little miracle,
Turning that water to wine,
A fruity shiraz, or full-bodied rioja,
Rather than additive-filled
Non-alcoholic
Wesleyan communion wine.
But even that would do to
Put flavour on my palate
Or rather to displace
The taste of putrefaction.

Putrefaction – there's a good word!
I savour that as I suck,
At the sponge on a stick,
Proving to my watchers
That I am still here;
Suckling in my closing hours
As I did when I entered the world.
It seems like only yesterday
I watched my children

Suckling in a hospital bed,
And here they are now watching me...

Or most of them are
He's not.
He's too busy.
As I once was.
My God, my God why did I forsake him
So that he has forsaken you?
Assure me that you have not
Forsaken him...
Just as I trust that you have not
Forsaken me in these last days.
Though it might seem
And feel that you have.
Could I have done more?
Should I have done less?
Into your hands I commit my questions.
Into your unseen hands I commit my spirit.
Into your unseen hands
And each other's care
I commit my loved ones.
I can do no more.
It is finished.

This long, rambling poem/monologue is the product of sleeplessness, reading a fictional account of the death of Jesus and Clive James's self-penned poem about impending death written in 2014, but widely shared on social media in the light of his demise on the 24th November 2019. Please don't seek to compare this to his piece - there is simply no comparison. He was a genius, and I do not use that word lightly. Also I should also say that the characters in this piece are not anyone living, dead or dying, although it is obviously influenced by my experience as a pastor, a relative of people who have been seriously ill and died in hospital and particularly as a chaplain for 14 years.

Reduced

Reflections on a Cremation

A life reduced to
Three lines in a newspaper obituary
Including dates of birth and death

A person reduced to
Twenty three minutes and no more
Including a few anecdotes and poems

A body reduced to
Ashes at the press of a button
To be scattered or interred if desired

A relationship reduced to
Redundant contact details
Persistently passed from phone to phone

A human being reduced to
Pixelated images on social media
Perhaps helpfully tagged

A love reduced to loss
Years wiped away with tears
Leaving a void in the memory

Loss and Gain

For Gerry and Dennis

Life is loss.
It's unavoidable.
But all loss is gain;
We simply must choose
The nature of the gain.
A callus on the heart;
A lacuna in the soul
Serving as a reservoir
Of resentment
And bitterness?
A constant reminder
Of things that never happened
And never will;
Of words left unspoken;
Wounds left unhealed.

Or if healed,
If chosen
A connection
With others in their loss
And pain.
Not knowing how they feel
But that they do feel
Or have lost
The capacity to feel for now
And need others to feel for them.

A connection
With a deeper sense of self,
Forced to grow into
The vacated space.
A growth that is
Frequently unkempt,
Chaotic,
But can be cultivated
To produce a fuller
More flavoursome harvest.

A connection
With that other world.
A sense of somewhere
Just out of reach;
On the periphery
Of sound and vision,
Peopled by
A cheering crowd
Of friends and family
Known
And, as of yet,
Unknown.

Another piece on death, dying and loss in part prompted by our annual service of remembrance for those who have died and been bereaved, but also reading the episode in Gladys Ganiel's biography of my friend and inspiration Gerry Reynolds, where when visiting the site of Marconi's historic transatlantic radio transmission at Clifden, he thanks God for the loss of his father in childhood, and other losses, because they gave him a sense of a communion with those no longer with us. That resonated with something that Gerry's friend and my former Theological college principal Dennis Cooke said to me after my own mother's death, which he had drawn from the death of his parents, that loss connects us, and imbues us with a longing for restored relationships.

Haven

Summer 2019

A safe place,
For those near the start
Of their journey,
Yet already bruised
By loss or rejection,
Sometimes not only
Bruised but
Broken,
Inside and out.

A safe place,
For those nearing the end
Of their journey,
Bodies often bruised
By a lifetime of memories
Good and not so good,
And with minds and memories,
Good and not so good,
Increasingly untethered
From what remains.

A haven is not
A permanent place.
It is a safe place to stay
For a time

This is the poem I mentioned in the introduction, prompted, as I said by the Copelands Elderly Care Facility and the Childhaven Home that previously stood on the same site. Some of the ideas behind this poem may be the seed for a longer dramatic project.

On a sometimes troubled sea
A place to rest a while
And watch the waves
Until it is time to take
The next leg of the journey.

All

November 1st 2019

All!
That great crowd of witnesses
Cheering us on to the final whistle
From the heavenly terraces.
Not just the sanctified celebrities,
But our unremembered, unrecognised,
Unhaloed predecessors,
Who filled pews and cleaned loos;
Lived their faith unfussily,
Passing it on by word and deed,
Not words proclaimed from pulpits,
But the quiet kind word
In the right place at the right time;
Not spectacular miraculous deeds,
But simple acts of grace
Far from the spotlight's glare.
Let's celebrate the uncelebrated.

All!
Not just the long departed,
Removed from this messy arena,
Encouraging us to come join them;
Not just those gloriously shining,
But our fellow feeble strugglers.
Those we recognise
As brothers and sisters
Because we think and speak
With the same theological accent;
Because we sing and dance (or not)
To the same spiritual tune,
But also estranged siblings

Living under different roofs,
Singing strange songs
And eating suspicious food,
Yet no less sanctified than us.

All saints.

Ride On

For John

Ride on brother, ride on
You've had a tough climb
You can now fill your lungs
Lift your head and ride on.

From the start you set the pace
Showed us what needed done
Encouraged those less able
And inspired all those around

You always cheered on others
Now your brothers and sisters
Of all generations and nations
Applaud your run for home

The victor's crown awaits you
We feebly struggle in your wake
But you never sought the glory
You just did what needed done

So now you've crested the hill
We've lost sight of you for now
But your example spurs us on
And we'll see you at the finish

Written in May 2019 on the death of John Stephens, a Methodist ministerial colleague who was a keen cyclist, after a relatively brief but tough battle with brain cancer. It has been previously published in the Methodist Newsletter and adapted as a song by Philip McKinley. It uses some of the same wording and analogies as the previous poem, demonstrating again my limitations and lack of originality. Ah well…

So ride on brother, ride on
You've had a tough climb
You can now fill your lungs
Lift your head and ride on.